Advance Praise

"The inspirational Chris Edmonds te...... ....o values aligned and high performance wisdom so we can connect the dots about corporate culture."

Lolly Daskal (@lollydaskal) is a speaker, facilitator, and coach who guides others to "Lead From Within."

"Whether you want to think about, learn about, or go about improving your organizational culture, you need this amazing little book!"

Kevin Eikenberry (@kevineikenberry) is a leadership expert, speaker, consultant, and author of several books including *From Bud to Boss*

"Chris' culture tweets are engaging, challenging reminders of how to create healthy, fun, energetic work environments. Read and be inspired!"

Becky Robinson (@beckyrbnsn) is a writer, social media consultant, and blogger at http://www.weavinginfluence.com

---

"Chris Edmonds is first a learner and then a teacher. His learner's spirit makes him a great teacher. It's great learning from him again."

Dan Rockwell (@leadershipfreak) is a community leader and consistent #leadership Top Tweet'er.

"Culture only changes through a consistent focus on what you want to achieve. These terrific ahas from Chris Edmonds will show you how!"

David Witt (@LeaderChat) is the marketing Program Director with The Ken Blanchard Companies

---

"Culture doesn't need to be a magic word. Chris Edmonds tells you how to make it work for you in 140 character bursts."

Wally Bock (@wallybock) helps leaders at all levels do a better job and live a better life.

"Only three things matter in business: culture, culture, culture. No one gets this key leadership lesson better than Chris Edmonds."

Ted Coiné (@tedcoine) is a business heretic and (un)CEO at http://www.savvycapitalist.blogspot.com.

"Chris Edmonds has hit the nail on the head with a timely, relevant, must-read book on corporate culture."

Laura Goodrich (@lauragoodrich) is a workforce innovator, filmmaker and author of *Seeing Red Cars and Shifting Years – Leverage the Power of Generations*

"A strong corporate culture makes all the difference! Chris Edmonds' new book #CORPORATE CULTURE tweet can help yours build its muscles."

Joan Koerber-Walker (@JKWleadership) is Founder and Chairman of CorePurpose, Inc.

"Essential reading for all leaders! Corporate culture guru Chris Edmonds shows you how to create a team where passion and performance reign."

Jesse Lyn Stoner (@jesselynstoner) is Founder of the Seapoint Center and Coauthor of *Full Steam Ahead! - Unleash the Power of Vision*

#CORPORATE CULTURE **tweet** Book01

140 Bite-Sized Ideas to Help You Create a High Performing,
Values-Aligned Workplace that Employees LOVE

By S. Chris Edmonds
Foreword by Ken Blanchard

E-mail: info@thinkaha.com
20660 Stevens Creek Blvd., Suite 210,
Cupertino, CA 95014

Published by *THiNKaha*®, a Happy About® imprint
20660 Stevens Creek Blvd., Suite 210, Cupertino, CA 95014
http://thinkaha.com

First Printing: April 2011
Paperback ISBN: 978-1-61699-048-0 (1-61699-048-1)
eBook ISBN: 978-1-61699-049-7 (1-61699-049-X)
Place of Publication: Silicon Valley, California, USA
Paperback Library of Congress Number: 2011926214

Trademarks

Warning and Disclaimer

Dedication

To my wife, Diane, and my family (especially Mom and Dad, Karin and Greg, and Andy and Dana), who keep me and our family culture on track with coaching, humor, and love.

This book is also dedicated to:

My best bosses (and worst bosses) who taught me more about the power of culture than any course could accomplish.

My culture clients, who accept my coaching with grace and enthusiasm while helping me understand how to personalize our culture change process to ensure traction.

My social media mentors, particularly Becky Robinson, Lolly Daskal, Kevin Eikenberry, and Dan Rockwell, who continue to guide and support me in that space.

Acknowledgments

Special thanks to my wife, Diane, for her love, support, and enthusiasm, all of which made this book possible. She tolerates me writing tweets and blog posts at all hours.

To my mentor and friend Becky Robinson, who championed my idea for this book when it was little more than an expressed thought.

To Ken Blanchard, Lolly Daskal, Becky Robinson, Kevin Eikenberry, Dan Rockwell, David Witt, Ted Coine, Jesse Lyn Stoner, Wally Bock, Laura Goodrich, and Joan Koerber-Walker for reviewing this book in its early stages and providing such kind praise.

To Mitchell Levy and the entire Happy About® team for their enthusiastic activity and support of the *#CORPORATE CULTURE tweet* addition to the *THiNKaha®* elite series.

Why Did I Write This Book?

I want to help leaders create less frustrating, more supportive work environments where goals are exceeded and staff *love* what they do.

I want to leverage my unique culture refinement expertise so that workplaces are energizing, effective places to live and work in.

I want to help leaders not only *think* about how to refine their organization, division, department, or team culture, but I want them to *act* on these tangible, proven practices.

S. Chris Edmonds
Senior Consulting Partner with the Ken Blanchard Companies
http://chris-edmonds.com
http://kenblanchard.com/edmonds
http://twitter.com/scedmonds
http://DrivingResultsThroughCulture.com
http://facebook.com/DrivingResultsThroughCulture
http://www.linkedin.com/profile/view?id=7202796

Contents

Help You Create a High Performing, Values-Aligned Workplace that Employees LOVE

Foreword by
Ken Blanchard

"Packed with wisdom, Chris Edmonds' bite-sized nuggets on corporate culture will make your organization healthy. Take at least one a day!"

Ken Blanchard (*@kenblanchard*) is the chief spiritual officer of the Ken Blanchard Companies and the mega-bestselling author of nearly 50 influential books, including *The One Minute Manager*®.

Section 1

What Is Culture?

Most leaders never think about their organization's culture, yet it has a powerful impact on employee performance and passion. The ahas that follow help define what a healthy workplace culture looks, acts, and sounds like.

1

How you treat your employees and customers tells me more about your values than anything posted on your walls.

2

How you manage your direct and indirect reports becomes dinner conversation with their families and friends each night.

3

A high performing, values-aligned culture requires senior leaders to be cheerleaders, role models, and teachers daily.

4

In order to maximize opportunity, you must align your company vision, purpose, values, goals, and strategies.

5

How do you describe your company
culture to acquaintances?
Is it a vibrant, fun, accomplished
place to work?

6

What does your company culture
reward? Performance at all costs
or performance with great
citizenship and service?

7

Does your culture enable great talent retention or erode it? Do you know what your top performers think about working there?

8

Do your company's leaders see their primary job as managing processes and results, or as managing people's energy?

9

Do daily plans, decisions, and actions align with your company's stated vision, purpose, values, and goals?

10

Does every player in your company have a clear performance plan which includes defined goals and values expectations?

11

Are your leaders seen as talented, credible believers in team members' success? Do they demonstrate trust and respect in every interaction?

12

Does every player understand what values and behaviors to demonstrate to be seen as a "great corporate citizen?"

13

Does every player know exactly what performance is expected of them every day and know how they're doing on each target?

14

The ways that leaders treat employees tell me exactly what your company values. Is your work environment fair and just?

15

Leaders can measure team members and team performance when clear goals exist. Without those, it is difficult for teams to gauge success.

16

Your employees do a *lot* of things right. To what extent are they "caught doing things well" by their leaders?

17

Does every interaction a leader has with his/her employees make them feel trusted, honored, and respected?

18

Effective, inspiring leaders "connect the dots" for employees. They clearly communicate strategy and link employee goals to that strategy.

19

Ask your employees: "What is the purpose of our company? Why do we exist?" Their answers may depress you. Inspire them with meaningful work!

20

Create a workplace of shared knowledge, skills, and insights. It increases the team's ability to contribute and satisfy customers' needs.

21

Unconditional Positive Regard: Act on the belief that your fellow humans are good, mean well, and contribute to your well-being and success.

22

Do you have an executive "team" or a "group" of leaders battling for limited funds, people, and resources? Build a *team* with a common goal.

23

Want to amp up your discretionary energy? Then work on building trust between and among team members in your organization

24

Leaders, please remember: Just because something is easy to measure does not make it the right thing to focus on.

25

Great bosses focus team energy on terrific service, growing efficiency, increasing performance, and genuine passion, every day.

26

Clear strategy and goals can help *every* team member align to the right targets. Clear values help staff do the right things the right way.

27

The values you demonstrate with every interaction are immensely powerful. Who are you *being* while doing what you do?

28

Celebrate team progress and accomplishments *regularly*. Praise and encourage the right decisions and actions and you'll see more of them!

29

Create a workplace with an

abundance mentality

(plenty for everyone) vs.

a scarcity mentality

(grab my piece *now*).

Abundance = satisfaction!

30

The most important thing on earth is the condition of our relationships with others. Ensure your culture improves relationships daily!

31

Always behave in ways that enable you to "hold your head high" at the end of each day: values aligned, progress made, relationships intact.

32

Do your employees

demonstrate passion?

Are they excited to get to

work, create with talented

peers, and have fun

serving customers?

33

Does your company serve

your community?

Seek friends/neighbors/

non-profits and ask,

"What can we help you with?"

Serve fifty hours per year.

34

A powerful "referral" effort exists re: your company's products, services, and interactions. Customers talk about the negative and positive.

35

Laughter among valued colleagues is a wonderful energy booster! Find ways to laugh *with* (not at) your team members today.

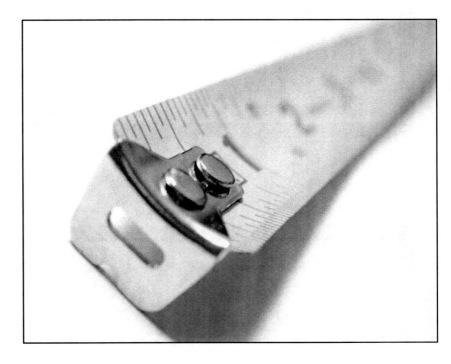

Section II

Creating Culture Standards

Most organization's cultures happen by default—not by design. The ahas in this section describe the requirement for clear performance standards, clear values standards (in the form of observable valued behaviors), and accountability for both.

36

Rise above the temptation to focus solely on performance! What values are acted on in your company today? Are those the values you *want*?

37

Goal clarity drives performance and confidence. List your top five goals in priority order. See if your boss agrees with your list and order!

38

Leaders, ask your team: What are the things that keep you from working efficiently? Remove those hurdles and see performance skyrocket!

39

Leaders, ask your team: "Are there things you see happening to customers that shouldn't?" Address those issues and customers will be wowed!

40

Your employees are your *first* customer; purchasers of your products/services are your *second* customers. Treat employees like *gold*.

41

Values-aligned leaders always own up to their mistakes and share learnings so others won't go down the same path.

42

Balance strategic leadership (vision, values, plans) with operational leadership (goals and tactics). Most spend 95% of time on operational.

43

Focus on what you *can* do to clarify expectations and hold staff accountable. Worry not about what you *cannot* do.

44

What misaligned activities and behaviors are you tolerating that inhibit high performance and values alignment across your team?

45

Clear work agreements drive performance and employee work passion. A lack of clear agreements drives inconsistent delivery and frustration.

46

Leaders, get your hands dirty!
Jump in to fulfill orders, listen
in on customer calls, go on
sales calls with your staff.
Learn what works!

47

Employees have rich lives: They are spouses, parents, volunteers, etc. Enable these responsibilities through balance and win their hearts.

48

Intelligent disobedience: when staff follow the rules unless it doesn't make sense! Have clear vision, values, goals—then let people *think*.

49

Clear vision, values, and goals enable leaders to praise progress, redirect when needed, and coach players who are not contributing.

50

Leaders, meet w/your team early today and map out this week's strategy: Each one talk to one of your key clients, live (not vmail). Connect!

51

Are you creating "satisfied" customers? Satisfied customers aren't necessarily loyal or devoted! "Wow" your customers to create devotion.

52

Check with your internal customers: Ask, "to be helpful, what do you need me to do more of, less of, or start doing?" Then, deliver!

53

What is your organization's purpose, its reason for being? If not formally defined, that purpose will be defined by activities alone.

54

Deliver promised products
and services with top quality,
on time, fair cost, and
no drama = you're a desired
teammate and provider!
No excuses.

55

Leaders, do you hold all staff equally accountable for performance and values expectations? If not, you erode trust, respect, and innovation.

56

Few people get up in the
morning with the hope
that they'll screw up a team
member's day. Stuff happens.
Trust and respect begets
trust and respect.

57

Watch for cooperation amongst team members. See it, praise it! If not seen, coach and encourage it. "All of us are smarter than one of us."

58

If you could view a video of last month's plans, decisions, and actions, would it show you were focused on profits, performance, or people?

59

How responsive are you?
How long does it take you to
return a vmail or email? Best
practice organizations ask
staff to do so in <24 hours.

60

To what extent do you contribute to staff performance problems? Lack of clear goals and inconsistent accountability are *big* contributors!

61

Unclear roles and responsibilities cost time, money, and human passion. Get clear agreements about who does what, and honor those agreements.

62

Create "cooperative interaction" among team members. Competition erodes relationships through "I win, you lose."

63

Great bosses are unafraid to tell team members "I don't know." Learning new skills and approaches is a priority.

64

Great contributors improve what and how they accomplish tasks every day. They do not wait for someone to tell them to do that!

65

Great bosses ensure their team has a clear understanding of the team's *compelling* and *inspiring* purpose. All members *know* it.

66

Great bosses don't delay addressing poor performance. They engage in conversations to verify the goal and coach to success.

67

Great contributors are willing learners. They cycle out skill sets that no longer serve and dive into building needed skills.

68

Great bosses ensure that every team member understands the positive impact of their contribution to team output.

69

Great contributors look out for their peers. They share information and best practices, jump in to help, and demonstrate care.

70

Great contributors work hard to keep their skill set current. They study, embracing best practices to improve efficiency.

Section III

Great Boss Behaviors

Most of us remember our best boss ever, a person who created a work environment that enabled us to perform at our best while being incredibly satisfied with our boss, our team, and our work. Ahas in this section describe how great bosses behave to ensure culture standards are acted upon each day.

71

Great bosses don't need an "open door policy." They manage by wandering around, engaging staff every day.

72

Leaders: Spend two hours a week connecting with select employees (F2F or virtual); ask what's going well and what's not. Then do what's asked.

73

Who are you? What are your values
and how do you act on them each day?
Are your values aligned with your
organization's values?

74

Leaders: hold 30-minute 1:1 meetings
with direct reports every 2 weeks.
NO AGENDA except to see what they
need & how they're doing.

75

Leaders: your job = manage performance *and* employee relationships. Performance success is good; effectiveness at managing both is *great*.

76

Great bosses deliver what they promise to internal and external customers; they do what they say they will do! No excuses.

77

Whether you believe your staff are "slackers" and mean harm or you believe your staff are high-performing "stars," you are right.

78

Great bosses are PRESENT.

They look team members

in the eye, listen, and learn

about opportunities

in their team.

79

Servant leaders inspire by modeling company values and catching people doing things right. Would your staff say you are their best boss ever?

80

We often apply the same solutions to unique issues and opportunities. Increase your "solution skills" by studying others' successes. Then try.

81

Primary job of a leader: Build trust. How do you know if your staff trusts you? *Ask them.* Big trust builder: Do what you say you will do.

82

Be consistent. Do what you say you will do. Meet deadlines. Exceed expectations. It takes time and energy, but it will change you for *good*.

83

To build trust between you and direct reports: Expect the best and give others the benefit of the doubt. Set clear goals, coach, and praise.

84

Communicate corrective messages so staff are drawn into the solution, not into a defensive stance about what created the problem.

85

Quick! Note your staff's "outside work" interests and names of their SOs, spouses, kids. Can't do that? Your work relationships needs *work*.

86

Don't know what your staff thinks of your recent plans, decisions, or actions? Amazing approach that enables work connections: *Ask them.*

87

Leaders, share business challenges and opportunities with staff. Engage their brains in problem solving. You'll see increased commitment!

88

Leaders are *nothing* without followers. Leaders are *amazing* when they create skilled, committed followers who love their customers.

89

Who you are and what you do speaks more loudly than what you say. Values-aligned leaders strive for consistency of words and action.

90

What did your best boss do daily to help you perform well and enjoy work and peers? What do your staff need from you to be their best boss?

91

How trusting of your staff are you? Have you delegated authority to make decisions in your absence, or do you touch every decision made?

92

Be a voice of optimism in your workplace. Look for what is going well, celebrate successes, challenge folks to ever higher accomplishments!

93

Leaders, everything you say and do is scrutinized in the workplace. Know that you are never "off duty."

94

Everything you do as a
leader either helps, hinders,
or hurts the creation of
a high performance,
values-aligned culture.

95

Leaders, you are role models whether you are aware of it or not. How do you respond in the heat of the moment: with caring concern or anger?

96

Leaders, are you *pleasant* and *present* when interacting with staff? If so, you build trust and respect. If not, you build suspicion and anxiety.

97

Err on the side of inclusion with plans, decisions, and actions that impact team members. Bring them "in" and buy-in will follow.

98

Great bosses aim for transparency. Share challenges and opportunities. Individuals make better decisions when "in the know."

99

Great bosses create an
environment where new
ideas and new markets
are considered—all while
WOW'ing current customers.

100

Great bosses don't settle for "great *today*." They ask team members to help them understand what great looks like *tomorrow*, too.

101

Great contributors scan their environment to learn better ways of partnering with clients and peers, every day.

102

Great bosses know aligning great contributors to team strategy is critical *and* know great contributors must be trusted to *act*.

103

Great bosses want *every* staff member thinking about how to increase quality and service levels, every day. Share and test ideas!

104

Great bosses trust and respect staff, every interaction, every day. There is no excuse for treating people as less than equals.

105

Great bosses leverage the power and responsibility they have to effectively manage staff members' heads, hearts, *and* hands.

Section IV

Sustaining Your Desired Culture

Culture change is hard—and it takes disciplined effort to focus on culture management day in and day out. The ahas in this section focus on accountability behaviors and actions that ensure your desired culture is embedded and acted upon.

106

Great bosses express sincere thanks to staff members for their specific contributions, every day. Practice "active praising!"

107

Call a customer today. Don't sell them anything. Ask how your company is doing and what you could do better. Fix issues and share insights.

108

Hold staff accountable for performance *and* values expectations. *How* they meet their goals is vitally important!

109

Crush stupid policies; they demotivate and create negative energy. Which policies are stupid? Ask your employees. They marvel at them daily.

110

Leaders: Do your team members understand how accomplishing their goals helps their department and, ultimately, the organization succeed?

111

Leaders: Each week, host an informal lunch forum with 6–8 random employees. Ask what's going well and what's not. Fix what's not ASAP!

112

Be calm and present today. Offer thanks for the good in others. Do a favor for another that will not be credited or returned.

113

Resolving performance
problems is about
1) a clear goal, 2) root causes
(the leader can be one!),
3) consequence management
to close gaps.

114

Leaders, do a mystery shopper call weekly. Call your facilities/offices and ask questions customers ask. You'll learn what's working, fast.

115

What about your work *inspires* you? Share that inspiration with your team— and ask each team member what inspires them. Focus on positives!

116

How do you respond to workplace gossip? A values-aligned leader knows that gossip erodes trust—nip it in the bud!

117

Values-aligned leaders don't "throw people under the bus." When issues arise, their heart assesses behaviors and decisions, not the person.

118

Communication creates community. If you want a laser-focused, values-aligned, high-performance work team, keep strategy and tactics clear.

119

To connect with your staff: 1) Place hands on desk 2) Push self away from computer 3) Stand 4) Walk and talk amongst staff. Cheer folks on!

120

Stay connected to company staff.
Weekly, do a focus group meeting/
meal and discuss, "What gets in the
way of performance and values?"

121

Is it OK for staff to be *learners* in
your organization? If not, they'll
mask their lack of competence.
Learning is a *good* thing—allow it!

122

Your staff know if a player isn't carrying their load. They don't blame the player as much as they blame their *boss.* Hold folks accountable!

123

Leaders, demonstrate support for development activities: Kick off classroom sessions in person, describing how new skills will serve!

124

If your plans, decisions, and actions are not consistent with stated strategy or values, you're frustrating and demotivating staff. Align!

125

Leaders, are you measuring, monitoring, and rewarding the *right* things in your company? Strategize what you need and reward those things.

126

What are you thankful for this week? Express gratitude for a project completed, a customer "wowed," a problem addressed. Takes only minutes!

127

Just like a sports team huddles to agree on a plan, your team should huddle (at least weekly) to discuss wins, issues, and opportunities.

128

Great bosses do not demonstrate self-serving behaviors or tolerate such behaviors from anyone in their organization.

129

Practice "planned spontaneous recognition." Decide daily what you'll look for from your team. See it, celebrate it, repeat!

130

Is yours a culture of praise and encouragement? You'll know it is when you see peers openly praising and thanking peers daily.

131

Individuals can only contribute their knowledge, skills, and passion when they truly understand your business strategy and vision.

132

Do front line employees on your team clearly act on both the strategy and the tactics agreed upon to accomplish that strategy?

133

Great bosses create a work culture where everyone leaves their shift safe and with "head held high" for jobs well done.

134

Great bosses actively manage their organizational culture. Every day they tour, touch base, and tell to reinforce their desired culture.

135

Does your culture inspire genuine trust, friendship, and collaboration? If not, you're losing time, talent, and treasure.

136

Great bosses act on their primary responsibility to *remove employee frustrations* in the workplace.

137

Great bosses are not great exclusively because they generate productivity— but because they also generate employee passion.

138

Great bosses look to engage staff in solutions—they can't know the exact right answer to every challenge.

139

Great companies change all the time—they refine strategies, tactics, markets. What *does not* change is their values base.

140

Profits are the applause you get from customers you WOW, day in/out. Only trusted and passionate employees will WOW customers consistently!

About the Author

S. Chris Edmonds is a speaker, author, and senior consultant with the Ken Blanchard Companies. Chris is co-author of Blanchard's bestselling book, *Leading At A Higher Level*, and co-author of Blanchard's award-winning culture change process. Chris is Blanchard's culture expert and has helped numerous clients create a high performing, values-aligned culture using their proven process. Chris has thousands of Twitter, Facebook, and LinkedIn followers who look forward to his culture tweets each day.

Chris is also a member of the Jones and Raine band, a recording artist for Graystone Records, based in Denver, CO.

Find Chris online at:
http://chris-edmonds.com
http://kenblanchard.com/edmonds
http://twitter.com/scedmonds
http://DrivingResultsThroughCulture.com
http://facebook.com/DrivingResultsThroughCulture
http://www.linkedin.com/profile/view?id=7202796

Music:
http://JonesandRaine.com
http://chris-edmonds-music.com

Other Books in the THiNKaha Series

The THiNKaha book series is for thinking adults who lack the time or desire to read long books, but want to improve themselves with knowledge of the most up-to-date subjects. THiNKaha is a leader in timely, cutting-edge books and mobile applications from relevant experts that provide valuable information in a fun, Twitter-brief format for a fast-paced world.

They are available online at http://thinkaha.com or at other online and physical bookstores.

1. *#BOOK TITLE tweet Book01:* 140 Bite-Sized Ideas for Compelling Article, Book, and Event Titles by Roger C. Parker

2. *#COACHING tweet Book01:* 140 Bite-Sized Insights On Making A Difference Through Executive Coaching by Sterling Lanier

3. *#CONTENT MARKETING tweet Book01:* 140 Bite-Sized Ideas to Create and Market Compelling Content by Ambal Balakrishnan

4. *#CORPORATE CULTURE tweet Book01:* 140 Bite-Sized Ideas to Help You Create a High Performing, Values Aligned Workplace that Employees LOVE by S. Chris Edmonds

5. *#CROWDSOURCING tweet Book01:* 140 Bite-Sized Ideas to Tap into the Wisdom of the Crowd by Kiruba Shankar and Mitchell Levy

6. *#DEATHtweet Book01:* A Well-Lived Life through 140 Perspectives on Death and Its Teachings by Timothy Tosta

7. *#DEATH tweet Book02:* 140 Perspectives on Being a Supportive Witness to the End of Life by Timothy Tosta

8. *#DIVERSITYtweet Book01:* Embracing the Growing Diversity in Our World by Deepika Bajaj

9. *#DREAMtweet Book01:* Inspirational Nuggets of Wisdom from a Rock and Roll Guru to Help You Live Your Dreams by Joe Heuer

10. *#ENTRY LEVEL tweet Book02:* Inspiration for New Professionals by Christine Ruff and Lori Ruff

11. *#ENTRYLEVELtweet Book01:* Taking Your Career from Classroom to Cubicle by Heather R. Huhman

12. *#IT OPERATIONS MANAGEMENT tweet Book01:* Managing Your IT Infrastructure in The Age of Complexity by Peter Spielvogel, Jon Haworth, Sonja Hickey

#CORPORATE CULTURE **tweet**